IMAGES OF ENGLAND

Around Honiton

Joe Lake, Honiton's town crier, in around 1953, with the glove which formed part of the ritual associated with the opening ceremony of Honiton fair. The crier played a leading role in the opening of the annual fair, which is known to have been held from at least 1221. Held on differing dates in earlier years, the fair is now held on the first Wednesday and Thursday after 19 July, when the Town Crier proceeds up High Street to the Old Market House carrying a stuffed glove on a flower-decked pole. He officially opened the fair at midday with a shout of 'Oyez! Oyez! Oyez!' and followed with these phrases which were also cried three times: 'The Glove Is Up! The Fair Is Begun! No Man Shall Be Arrested! Until The Glove Is Taken Down! God Save the Queen!' The reference to immunity to arrest only referred to debtors. After the ceremony the glove was placed in front of the Kings Arms and, following that pub's closure in 1975, the Angel during the cattle fair. When the Angel was closed, the glove was placed in front of the New Dolphin Hotel. The following day (the horse fair) it was taken to the White Lion, the inn closest to site of the horse fair. Among the spectators here are Jimmy Bowden and Mrs Lovering with her two daughters.

IMAGES OF ENGLAND

Around Honiton

Les Berry
and
Gerald Gosling

NONSUCH

For the staff at Lisburne, past and present

First published 1995
This new pocket edition 2005
Images unchanged from first edition

Nonsuch Publishing Limited
The Mill, Brimscombe Port,
Stroud, Gloucestershire, GL5 2QG
www.nonsuch-publishing.com

British Library Cataloguing in Publication Data.
A catalogue record for this book is available from the British Library.

ISBN 1-84588-152-4

Typesetting and origination by Nonsuch Publishing Limited
Printed in Great Britain by Oaklands Book Services Limited

Contents

Tom Bambury was one of Honiton's best-known businessmen, working in the grocery trade in the High Street for over fifty years. Leaving school aged thirteen, he began work as an errand boy for Mr W.H. Foale at his High Street grocers shop on 1 June 1915. His starting wage was a princely three shillings and six pence a week, for which he began work at eight in the morning and worked until eight in the evening (ten on Saturdays). In later years he would recall that he did not have the traditional errand boy's bicycle but pushed a wheelbarrow full of orders as far as Tower Cross, Combe Raleigh or Tracey. The Christmas period was a particularly busy one, beginning six weeks before when things like dates, biscuits, sugar, etc. had to be weighed by hand. After his first year he got a rise of sixpence and went to work behind the counter. In 1922 he became manager, first for Mr Foale, then, when Mr Foale died in 1928, for Mrs Foale. In 1934, when Mrs Foale died and half the premises were bought as a butchers, Tom bought the other half and ran his own popular grocery business until 1967 when he retired – fifty-two years after he went there as the errand boy. His wife Alice, whom he married in 1932, helped in the business. He died in 1989.

Introduction

Honiton, the gateway to the west!

Writing in 1903, W.G. Willis Watson said that 'Honiton is situated in one of the most charmingly picturesque districts in the County of Devonshire... The locality for gracefulness and pleasing scenery has been compared with Italy.'

No doubt he was being effusive and, as a Honitonian, I can be accused of bias, but Honiton is an attractive town, set in a wide valley bounded on three sides by Gittisham Hill to the south, Dumpdon Hill to the east, and Hembury Fort to the north in a designated area of great natural beauty.

Nevertheless, there is more to the town than its looks. Its long history can be discovered from its interesting streets. The Dumnonii tribe were here before the Romans built their road along what is now the High Street. This was the main east–west route until the by-pass was constructed in the 1960s.

Hinastun, a Saxon farm, probably gave the town its name and the settlement developed in the area around St Michael's church. It has been said that there was a connection with the production of honey, hence 'Honeyton'. In the twelfth century, the Lord of the Manor, William de Redvers, decided to build a new town. He divided the land on both sides of the Roman road into long, narrow plots and erected houses. Disastrous fire and rebuilding changed the look of these houses, but the long narrow plots are still there behind the High Street facade.

Honiton was created a borough in 1300, and from the seventeenth until the nineteenth century sent two members to Parliament. The town's Parliamentary history was infamous for its corruption until the Reform Act established a wider franchise which brought about an alteration in the constituency boundaries.

The market is even older, dating from at least the reign of King John (1199–1216). The cattle market takes place in Silver Street but stalls still line the broad High Street on Tuesdays and Saturdays. Street markets are also held annually at the Honiton Fair on the first Wednesday after the 19th of July.

St Paul's church, built in 1837 in the Norman style, is perhaps a little out of place in a High Street of fine Georgian frontages. Next to St Paul's still stands Allhallows Museum, part of the original chapel of ease which came to be used by the townsfolk who chose not to climb the steep hill to St Michael's.

There are many buildings of special note. Allhallows is the oldest; New Street and High Street still have thatched properties; St Margaret's, at the west end of the town, was once a lepers' hospital; Marwood House was built in 1611 and is little changed; the Angel and the Dolphin were coaching inns, and Copper Castle was where the coachmen paid their tolls to use the turnpike road.

Old photographs and postcards have a nostalgic charm of their own and can bring the last hundred years of history closer than the written word. I congratulate Les Berry and Gerald Gosling on their book which brings some of Honiton's history to life.

Nan Steel, May 1995

One

Honiton – the Town

Honiton High Street decorated for the Celebration of Peace (for the Crimean War) on 29 May 1856. The print was dedicated to the Mayor, Samuel Devenish, by 'his obedient servant James Martin'. St Paul's church, in the background, was only consecrated eighteen years earlier.

The Shambles, Honiton, from an early print (It bears the date 1705 on the rear but that is open to question). Honiton's shambles were demolished in 1823, no doubt to the great relief of the stage coach drivers (on the right), who would have had some difficulty in threading their way through, especially on market days.

High Street, Honiton, c. 1745. The lady with the parasol would have a rude awakening (or worse) if she tried to stand in the same spot today!

High Street, Honiton, *c.* 1745, looking east.

Marwood House, High Street, Honiton, *c.* 1904. Marwood was built in 1619 by John Marwood, the son of Thomas Marwood, who was physician to Elizabeth I and famous for curing the Earl of Essex at a time when all the best London doctors had failed. He was a fine advert for his medical skills, living to 105 and practising as a doctor for seventy-five of them. John was also a doctor, as was his son, another Thomas, who, an ardent Royalist, entertained Charles I at Marwood House in 1644.

Honor Wilkinson (left) and Miss Stevens opposite the foot of Axminster Hill (now Kings Road), Honiton, September 1896. The wall and railings on the right are not all that different today, but the handsome tree on the right, along with the cottages immediately behind it, have gone to make way for more modern housing.

The junction of High Street and Axminster Hill (Kings Road), Honiton, in 1896. The railings and wall on the left, and the hedge on the right, have gone and housing development has taken place on both sides of the road.

Honiton's town centre was awash with flags, bunting and specially planted fir trees on 22 June 1897 to mark Queen Victoria's Diamond Jubilee. Even the outskirts had a sprinkling, as seen here near the top end of High Street.

High Street, Honiton, c. 1900.

Copper Castle, Honiton, *c.* 1900. The crenellated former toll-house on the edge of the town on Honiton Hill was built as a result of the Honiton Paving Act (1790), which was passed in Parliament to raise money for the improvement of the roads (mainly the through-coach road) in the town. In all seven toll-houses were built around the town, all becoming redundant when another Act of Parliament (1910) did away with tolls. Three of Honiton's seven remain, Copper Castle being the only one still with its gates. As the result of subsequent road widening, they would not meet in the middle if closed today.

Bramble Hill Toll Gate Honiton

Not all of Honiton's toll-houses were as substantial as 'Copper Castle' but were simple huts provided to give the gateman some shelter in bad weather. The hut at Bramble Hill (above), where the old Roman road drives arrow-straight into Honiton, could even be taken away. At the other end of the town, at Holy Shute (below), the hut seems to be of a more permanent nature. Both cards, dated around the turn of the century, were, unlike many of the old cards shown in this book which were printed or trademarked in the town, produced in Belgium.

Holy Shute, Toll Gate

High Street, Honiton, *c.* 1899.

High Street, Honiton, *c.* 1900. Some of the staff at Mr Harris's bakery have come outside for a photograph.

16

The Red Cow, High Street, Honiton, is seen here around 1910. The original building dates from at least 1795.

High Street, Honiton, looking east around 1908.

High Street, Honiton, *c.* 1904.

High Street, Honiton.

High Street, Honiton, in the 1930s. The parked cars would bring a smile to the face of today's traffic warden. Note that the coach was able to bring its passengers right to the door of 'Ye Honiton Lace Shoppe' and to that of the Carlton Café next door.

'Ye Honiton Lace Shoppe' in Honiton's High Street in the 1930s, with the then Carlton Café. It is not known for sure when the lace industry came to Honiton, but the middle of the sixteenth century is the generally accepted time. Like so many industries, mechanisation eventually killed off the hand-made trade, and despite many orders from the Royal Family, not least Queen Victoria's wedding lace, lace making in Honiton survives only as a craft. At the turn of the century the only lace shop remaining in the town was that belonging to Mrs Ann Fowler (see p. 67), but the above shop was opened in 1926. The Allhallows Museum next to St Paul's church has a large section dedicated to Honiton Lace and is well worth a visit.

The Dolphin Hotel, Honiton, seen above in 1903, was Honiton's premier hotel in the coaching era, but had already changed to accommodate the age of the motor car when this picture was taken, even if it still proudly parades its horse-drawn carriages, including its omnibus that 'meets all trains'. Below, by 1927 the motor age had definitely arrived. Built certainly as early as the mid-seventeenth century, the hotel was destroyed by fire in 1777. After refurbishment in 1958–59 the Dolphin became the New Dolphin.

High Street, Honiton, c. 1920. The old cinema can be seen on the right.

Of interest in this view of High Street taken around 1903 is the old White Hart Inn and the just visible gate and railings in front of St Paul's church. The latter vanished during a World War Two salvage drive.

High Street, Honiton, *c.* 1906.

High Street, Honiton. It is surprising to see just what a hold the motor car (and motor cycle) had taken on Honiton by the time this picture was taken in the mid-1920s. Vehicles are parked everywhere, and two of the town's garages, Cowells on the left and Moor's on the right, with their swinging-arm petrol pumps over the pavement, face each other across the road. Moor's, offering the services supplied by a garage, is flanked by 'good accommodation for the tourist'. Cowells later became Jack Sansom's cycle shop and was then taken over by Moor's. Today it is Huxtable's estate agents.

High Street, Honiton, *c.* 1902

The White Hart, High Street, Honiton, *c.* 1903.

Nearer the present day, a 1970s picture of High Street at its junction with New Street taken for traffic census purposes shows how many business premises have changed hands even in recent years, including both Key Markets and Abbotts.

Honiton, c. 1905, with the Fair Ground in the immediate foreground. The tall building in the middle background is the old National School, now flats.

East End, Honiton, c. 1913.

Elm Terrace, Clapper Lane, Honiton, c. 1903. W.E. Berry, the well-known Honiton photographer and picture framer, many of whose pictures appear in this book, lived and worked in the terrace.

New Street, Honiton, *c.* 1915.

New Street, Honiton, *c.* 1905. The Methodist Church (right) is now the Senior Citizens Centre, the Methodists having moved to a new chapel in, appropiately, Chapel Street. The iron railings in front went during a salvage drive in World War Two.

New Street, Honiton, before the railway bridge was built in the 1860s.

New Street, Honiton, c. 1901.

New Street, Honiton, *c.* 1909.

Frisby's Shoe Stores, High Street, Honiton, 1933.

Honiton High Street, looking west in around 1933. R.J. Lemon (right) was a well-known radio shop at the time.

High Street, West End, Honiton.

High Street, West End, Honiton, c. 1909. Of special interest is Haig's Globe Inn at the junction with Dowell Street, which sadly closed as recently as 1972 and became a private residence. Today it is the Society of Friends' Meeting Place. At different times in its history it was also known as both the Carpenter's Arms and the Three Compasses.

High Street, West End, Honiton, *c.* 1904. The Anchor Inn (right), immediately behind the bridge over the Gissage stream, closed in 1913, although the building still stands, as can be seen from the picture below (1959). In the later picture the Devonia Cinema can be seen on the left and the iron safety-railings, one of the more sensible of the modern age's 'improvements' in High Street, have arrived. The cinema burnt down in the 1960s and is now Taylor's saleroom. The board on the left in the top picture is above Joe Summers' general stores.

THATCHED COTTAGES, HIGH STREET, HONITON.

Bramble Hill, Honiton, *c.* 1910.

Bramble Hill, Honiton, looking into the town, *c.* 1930.

West End, Honiton, looking eastwards, *c.* 1899.

Rectory Gate, Honiton, *c.* 1904, looking down Bramble Hill into West End and High Street. Sadly, perhaps, the handsome gates are no longer, and even the rectory has become Rookswood Flats.

Allhallows' School, Honiton, *c.* 1903. The school's foundation date is unknown, but Allhallows Museum, once the schoolroom, has, according to J.R.W. Coxhead, 'the original cast window of the early fourteenth-century Chapel of Allhallows ... and a large portion of original stonework exists in the eastern part of the building.' *Bates* (1903) claims that schoolhouse and schoolroom must have suffered in the disastrous fire in 1765 which destroyed 180 houses as far as Clapper Lane. The schoolroom seen here was opened in 1770 but, after use as a dining room, was converted into a chapel in 1903. Soon after the school moved to Rousdon in 1938, it served as an ARP post during World War Two. In 1946 it was purchased by the museum's trustees. The picture below shows the school's playground.

Allhallows School House and the Dining Hall, Honiton, *c.* 1920.

The gymnasium, library and the new science laboratory, Allhallows School, Honiton, *c.* 1920.

34

Allhallows School Playing Fields, Honiton, c. 1926. Northcote Lane runs along the other side of the hedge on the left.

The Almshouses, Honiton.

The Almshouses (St Margaret's Hospital), Exeter Road, Honiton, c. 1905. Known to have existed as a leper hospital before 1374, it was rebuilt by Thomas Chard Lacey around 1530 and refounded as almshouses. Today the houses to the south of the road have become a meeing place for the Jehovah Witnesses.

Honiton from Littletown in the early 1920s, with the Fair Ground in the background. Honiton Bowling Club now occupy one of the fields on the left. The smallholding in the foreground has long since been demolished.

Littletown, Honiton, and the County Rifle Range (centre background), c. 1895.

Church Hill, Honiton, *c.* 1911. The fields on the left, now built on, were once part of Mr Tratt's farm.

Honiton Station entrance, looking into Church Hill, *c.* 1909.

Littletown Bridge, Honiton, c. 1925. It is hard to equate this idyllic rural scene with today's bustling Whitebridges estate, almost every blade of grass having been built on in recent years.

Littletown, Honiton, c. 1912, taken from just above the pony and trap in the picture above but looking in the opposite direction.

St Michael's church, Honiton, seen above in around 1905, is the former parish church. It was built in fits and starts in the fifteenth century and was severely damaged and gutted by fire on the morning of Sunday 11 March 1911 (below). It had been replaced as the parish church by St Paul's in 1835 and was constituted a chapel of ease. St Michael's position at the top of Church Hill meant a long hard climb for many worshippers, especially the old and the infirm, and it was also rather on the small side considering the population it was supposed to cater for.

HONITON CHURCH DESTROYED BY FIRE MAR 26 IX 11. COPYRD H

The Turk's Head Road House, *c.* 1936, formerly the Turk's Head public house. In later years it became Kastner's Garage and is now a horticultural shop.

B. Dyer's chemist shop, at the corner of Honiton's High Street and Northcote Lane, *c.* 1935. Today both Dyer's and next-door's Frisby's Shoe Stores are empty.

Two

Honiton – the People

Who the young soldier was, or what he was doing in Honiton towards the end of the nineteenth century, is not now known. Miller & Lilley, however, could well have sold him the feed for the horse. Long-established in the town, in those early days they could be found at Westcott House, just below the railway station. They have occupied premises in the High Street and the lower end of New Street in more recent years, before moving to a modern depot near the railway station which has subsequently been purchased by Bradford & Son, the Yeovil-based builders and agricultural merchants.

Left: Emily Gigg outside her tobacconist shop and gents' hairdressers shop in New Street, Honiton, 15 January 1924. The shop was demolished along with neighbouring premises, including the Black Lion Inn, when the lower end of New Street was widened in July 1970. The barber's pole is still in Honiton and in the family's hands. In some old pictures of New Street dating from the turn of the century there appear to be two barbers in New Street or, at least, two barber's poles.

Below: Honiton Pottery workers at the rear of the firm's High Street show room, *c.* 1955. Back row, left to right: Doris Brown, Jean Norman, Enid Trout (behind), Beryl Radford (behind), Joan Elston, Mrs Fookes (behind), Kay Richards. Front: May Ebdon, Jessie Bambury, Hilary Joy, Mollie Ebdon, Diana Chown, Nora Norman.

The parade enters St Paul's church, Honiton, for the Memorial Service for King George V in 1936.

Proclamation of King George V outside the Pannier Market, Honiton, 9 May 1910. Just over a year later Honiton was *en fête* for the new King's coronation on 22 June 1911. Proceedings began as early as 6 a.m., when the Town Band paraded around the town. At 9 a.m. all children under 14 received mugs outside St Paul's church, followed, an hour later, by the parade which formed at Bramble Hill and marched to church. In the afternoon the new fire engine was formally presented to the town and this was followed by a public tea for everyone in the High Street.

Left: George Lewis, who lived in St Cyres Road, Honiton, is seen here shortly after joining the Devonshire Regiment in the early 1920s. He saw service in India and, at the end of World War Two, was among the first men to enter the notorious Belsen concentration camp when it was liberated in 1945.

Below: Staff outside Dyer's chemist shop on the corner of Northcote Lane and High Street in 1946. Left to right: Peggy Marshall, Jean Manfield, -?-, Lorna Compton.

Among the many street parties held in Honiton to celebrate VE Day was this one in Queen Street. Among the children are Doreen and Mary Bambury, Jennifer Doble, Margaret Humphreys, Robert Dimond, Cyril Pike, Edwin Neighbours, Hune Godfrey and John Stoodley.

Milestones – such as finishing one's apprenticeship – were usually marked in pre-war Dimond & Co.'s High Street printers works with dressing up and a general 'ragging' of the happy man.

Joe Lake, the town crier, outside the Dolphin Hotel in the 1920s.

Joe Lake marches towards the Kings Arms to open a Honiton Fair in the 1930s. The old pannier market, to the left of the Dolphin Hotel, was occupied then by John W. Halse; later J.H. Slade & Son, the corn and coal merchant, had his premises there. Later still, it became Honiton's short-lived Woolworths branch. Among the spectators are Beat Bowen, Mrs Trembeth and Mrs Swift.

Children scramble for hot pennies thrown from the upstairs windows of the Kings Arms inn in Honiton's High Street as part of the time-honoured traditions of Honiton Fair. The penny-throwing tradition is said to have originated when some of the 'better classes' threw the near red-hot coins out of the windows and obtained cheap amusement from watching children trying to pick them up. Today the coins are nowhere near as hot. The White Horse in the top picture, which is dated around 1906, sadly closed in 1937. It was at the junction of High Street and Silver Street. Hill and Purse was a small general grocery store; C.P. Slade were engineers and ironmongers. The bottom picture is from the 1950s.

Coronation celebrations for King George VI (1937) in Honiton's Queen Street.

Honiton Borough Police shortly after the Borough Police Act (1856) required boroughs to have a regular force. The sergeant's garden was behind the wall and his cottage on the right. The men are seen here at the rear of the site of today's police station.

Two famous names from East Devon's political past. Morrison Bell (Conservative, 17,911) and Halse (Liberal, 16,353) can be seen on the placard in the upstairs window of the old police station which gives the result of the 1929 General Election. Mr Davis, with 913 votes, was presumably the Labour candidate. In older days, successful candidates were chaired by their supporters from the old Market Cross, which stood towards the eastern end of High Street, back to their headquarters. Honiton was a Conservative seat but never a safe one during the Liberal party's days of pomp. When created a borough by Edward I, the town elected two members of Parliament. The first, in 1301, were Galfridus Toleiner and Johannes de Swengethul, the latter sitting until 1311, when there was a break of over 300 years before Sir Walter William Pole and Walter Yonge were elected in 1640. The Redistribution of Seats Bill of 1885 saw Honiton's representation reduced to a single seat. Sir Peter Emery, the last member for the Honiton constituency before Honiton was added to the Triverton constituency, which was renamed the Triverton & Honiton constituency would, with an electorate of some 60,000, soon have been bankrupt if he had to follow the practice of a Mr Bradshaw who, in 1805, gave every voter six guineas after each election. A year later Lord Cochrane upped the 'bribe/thank-you' gift to ten guineas. The police station seen here was replaced by today's building, which stands further back from the road.

Although Honiton photographer W.E. Berry has written '... distribution of King George V Coronation Mugs by the Mayor Mr Seaborne Hook in 1911' on the reverse of this picture, the mugs are suspiciously like those given at the time of the 1919 Peace Celebrations; Mr Hook was mayor in both years.

Today's inspectors, bent on infringements of hygiene standards, would probably blanche at the sight of a whole side of beef and other meats exposed to passing dogs, flies, dust and God's free air. But no one attending Honiton's market in around 1890 was particularly worried.

The play *Princess Ju-Ju*, produced by Mrs Shepherd (then a teacher at the Honiton School) in about 1909.

Any Questions? held at Honiton School in the 1950s, with the Revd Fane de Sallis, Mrs Fane de Sallis, Mr and Mrs Owen Griffin, Les Shute, Mona Ayres, Alice Bambury, Gladys Lewis, Rose Lewis, Elsie Dyer, Mrs Baker, Mrs Aggett, Doreen Aggett, Mrs Penwarden, Mrs Warren, Mrs Rosewell and Mrs Clayton among the audience.

Left: Honiton Boy Scouts in 1928.

Below: Honiton Boy Scouts outside their Dowell Street HQ in the 1950s include Keith Sheppard and Rodney Pidgeon.

The 1st Honiton Boy Scout Troop, 1936, outside the Allhallows Playing Fields pavilion.

The dedication of the 1st Honiton Scout Troop's flag in 1935. Formed in 1910, the troop was not registered until 1922, and met during the early days in King Street opposite the entrance to Streamers Meadows. They have been in their Dowell Street HQ since 1935; the hall, given by Mr F. Cottrell, once stood on the site of the old prison.

'Stil' was a famous West Country cartoonist, associated on either side of World War Two with the *Express and Echo* and the *Western Times & Gazette*. His 1938 impressions of members of Honiton Bowling Club is of interest, if only for its inclusion of several prominent citizens of the time. These include Mr E. Hellier, the owner of Honiton Garage, Archie Dimond, the printer, George Cox, a local builder, Bob Delve, who ran the well-known electrical business, J.J. Carver, manager at Lloyds Bank, Jim Hoskins, the High Street draper, and F.G. Pollard, his partner.

Right: Charles George Lewis, who lived at Poplar Cottage in Honiton, spent twenty-five years of his working life with Dimond & Co, the High Street printers. A member of the Ancient Order of Foresters and the RAOB, he was a well-known and respected man in the town in which his death, in 1934 at the age of 54, was widely felt.

Below: Honiton Cricket Club annual dinner, held at the London Inn, Ottery St Mary, *c.* 1956. Standing, left to right: Reg Cann, Mrs Cann, Roy Edgecombe, Mrs P. Heard, Dave Pulman, Mary Pulman, -?-, Eddie Marks, Denis Hill, -?-, George Strawbridge, Peter Toogood, Marion Gosling, Mike Strawbridge. Sitting: Mr and Mrs Shobrooke (Torquay Corinthians), Mrs Strawbridge, Vic Strawbridge, Richard Whiteway (Whimple CC), Michael Kenwood, Brian Ward.

Left: Town crier Joe Lake outside the old Kings Arms inn in around 1953. Of interest is Delves in the background, with staff members on the roof watching the proceedings. The Town Crier's position has been occupied by a member of the Lake family from 1902–99. Today the position is held by Dave Ritter.

Below: Honiton Parish Church Choir outside St Paul's church, 1952. Back row, left to right: B.M. Davis, W. Norman, H. Dean, J. Helliar, M. Pulman, J. Lonsdale, Revd A. Fane de Salis (rector), R. Gallard, L.E. Helliar, E. Sparkes, D.S. Connett, D.P. Hann. Middle: W.S. Turner, A.G. Real, E. Clapp, A. Dimond, H.E. Carnell, A. Wyatt, H. Gollop, B. Dyer, W.H. Barnes. Front: W.T. Collins, M.L. Oliver, T. Jenkins, B.W. Underwood, D.M. Lane, R.S.C. Matthews, D.C.L. Ely, D.F. Hall, R. Hann, P.H. Rattenbury, B.H. Pulman.

Three

At Work ...

Ann Fowler, with the help of her two nieces, Misses B.D. and G.L. Ward, made much of the lace that was repeatedly favoured by royal warrants and, as stated on this 1903 advertisement, did so 'by Special Appointment to Queen Mary, Queen Alexandra and the late Queen Victoria'.

Left: Henry Langelaan, seen here modelling a Boy Scout on an advertisement in a 1908 Devon guide book, was a stone and marble worker of considerable repute in the West Country in Edwardian days. He was based at his appropriately named Memorial Works in New Street close to the railway station.

Below: Workmen unloading the plinth of Honiton's War Memorial prior to its erection in front of St Paul's church, c. 1920.

C.Harding and Son, who, having been established in Honiton's High Street as far back as 1815, were among the town's oldest businesses. Although mainly drapers, tailors and outfitters, they were also agents for the Devon and Exeter Savings Bank and for the 'celebrated' Naumann's Sewing Marchines, which, at the time of this picture (1913), could be purchased for as little as £2 15s. Note the display of hats in the second window from the left. The pictures below, from inside the shop, are of the Drapery (left) and Tailoring departments. Harding's were wholesale as well as retail tailors.

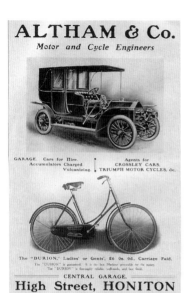

ALTHAM & Co.
Motor and Cycle Engineers

GARAGE. Cars for Hire.   Agents for
    Accumulators Charged.   CROSSLEY CARS.
        Vulcanizing.   TRIUMPH MOTOR CYCLES, &c.

The "DURION," Ladies' or Gents', £6 0s. 0d., Carriage Paid.

The "DURION" is guaranteed. It is the best Machine procurable for the money.
The "DURION" is thoroughly reliable, well-made, and best finish.

CENTRAL GARAGE,
High Street, HONITON

Left: Altham & Co, motor and cycle engineers at Central Garage, High Street, Honiton, in a 1903 advert.

Below: A.H. Baker, High Street, Honiton, *c.* 1906. Baker's were ironmongers who advertised at the time that they 'had every household requisite in stock ... prices were right ... quality could not be superseded ... and [they] had a good selection of oil cooking stoves (rare coal savers)'.

Mr and Mrs Robert Dimond outside the printers and stationers business they founded in Honiton's High Street in 1888. The top picture was taken around that time; the one below, which also shows Tom Bambury's grocery shop to the right, is from the early 1930s. Today the business is run by a fourth generation of the family, Robert Dimond's son Archie, his grandson Arthur, and now his great-grandson Anthony, all following him. Of interest in the bottom picture is the bicycle propped against the telegraph post. It belonged to a customer of many years standing who always propped it against the same post when he called for his daily paper. One day the pole was removed and the bewildered man wandered around not sure what was missing or where he could put his beloved bike.

Honiton Pottery, c. 1933. Left to right: Ern Carnell, Bert Nott and Walter Flood.

Fred Jeanes working with a potter's wheel at Honiton Pottery around 1925.

Decorators at work (above) at Honiton Pottery in the 1930s are, back row, left to right: Joan Collard (standing), Beryl Radford, Edith Redhead, Linda Marks, Dorothy Channon, Vera Stuart. Front: Peggy Cooper, Florrie Loving, Jessie Banbury. Below, around 1955, painting room staff are, left to right: Diana Chown, Joyce Turner, Mary Ebdon, Joan Barker, Carol Holton, Nora Norman, Mollie Ebdon, Gwen Sexton, Bill Crane (behind), Peggy Sevelle, Janet Manley (behind), Hilda Trout, Jean Norman. When the pottery industry began in Honiton is not now known, but it certainly existed by 1643, according to the Honiton Churchwarden's Accounts as quoted in J.R.W. Coxhead's celebrated 1984 book, *Honiton – A History of the Manor and the Borough*. James Webber built the pottery at the eastern end of High Street in 1881. It was later owned by Charles Collard (1918–47), who still used clay from a seam behind the Pottery. The present owner, Keith Luxton, continued production until 1991, when, following efforts to relocate the pottery because of the difficulty of expansion, production was transferred to Dartmouth Pottery, who, happily, retain the Honiton Pottery name for the products sold in the High Street show room. The old pottery, behind the show rooms, was demolished to make way for flats.

Market Day, Honiton, *c.* 1910. Pubs such as the Three Tuns (centre) did a roaring trade on market days.

Honiton Market in High Street, *c.* 1900. Of interest are the casually tended cattle, any one of which could (and probably often did) bolt down High Street.

Market Day, Honiton, at the turn of the century. Of interest are the shops with their handsome gas lamps (gas having come to Honiton in 1835), but the charm of this picture lies in the serenity of the handsome Georgian buildings that flank High Street, a blessing (although, no doubt, well disguised at the time!) to come out of disastrous eighteenth-century fires.

Market Day in Honiton's High Street, as seen here in around 1905, was the highlight of the week when East Devon's equivalent of the 'world and his wife' came to town. Circumstances, among them the embryonic motor age, led to the livestock market's moving away from the streets in 1910. The stalls stayed out, of course, and are still there – albeit with vastly different types of produce on offer.

As seen from the pictures on pages 64-65, Honiton's street market and the motor car did not mix, and the increase in motor traffic in Edwardian times led to the building of a new cattle market at the end of Silver Street, seen here on its opening day on 8 October 1910.

The motor age may have led to the opening of a new market in Honiton, but it also contributed towards its semi-demise, trade falling from the 1960s onwards, as more and more farmers found it easier to attend the bigger markets at Taunton and Exeter. Here, in around 1954, however, there was considerable interest in the Fat Stock Show.

Mrs Fowler proudly displays the royal warrant above her High Street lace shop, seen above in around 1903, by virtue of her 'special appointment to Her Most Gracious Majesty the Queen' (Alexandra); she was also patronised by HRH Princess of Wales (later Queen Mary), HRH Princess Louise and HRH Duchess of Teck. She later moved to premises (below) at the far eastern end of High Street, taking her appointment sign with her. The strangely shaped shop is still there, albeit now an optometrist. Mrs Fowler took over the business from a Mr Davey who held a royal warrant from Queen Adelaide (wife of William IV, 1830–37).

This postcard, although obviously from the 1930s, was posted to Ipswich in August 1952, at a time when the shop seems to have had a good season. The writer says, 'Unfortunately, all the small pieces, such as hankerchiefs with Honiton Lace on them, are sold out for this season.'

Matthews, Honiton's leading ironmongers when this picture was taken of their High Street shop in 1903, also had two shops in Axminster, one on the corner of Lyme Street and South Street, the other in Chard Street. It is interesting to note that all three sold petrol in cans. Petrol pumps were not introduced into Great Britain until 1920, when the AA operated a few in an attempt to get the oil companies to do the same. Once they had made their point and petrol pump equipped stations appeared, the AA closed theirs.

J. Compton, High Street, Honiton, 1903.

The Angel Hotel, High Street, Honiton, in the early 1930s (the school warning traffic sign places it before 1938, when Allhallows School moved to Rousdon). Honiton Fire Station was at the back of the hotel, as the sign above the old entrance to the stables indicates. Previously it had been in the Market House. The Angel dates from at least 1605 and had had a colourful history by the time Ralph Durbin Sprake (left) became licensee in 1916. He died in 1956, his wife taking over until she retired in 1965. Sold by the brewers (Bass Charrington) as a free house in 1973, it has now been developed as shops and apartments.

Right: Acland's Curio and Fancy Shop, Market Place, Honiton, *c.* 1925.

Below: George Blay Ltd, Marlpits Lane, Honiton, *c.* 1952. The five-acre timber yard and sawmill has been part of Honiton's industrial life since the middle of the nineteenth century. It came into George Blay's hands in 1917, when the mill machinery was steam-driven and transport and haulage was provided from the firm's own stables, which housed twenty-six horses. In 1936 they became a limited company, with John Maeer as their first managing director. The outbreak of World War Two saw the company encouraged to step up production, but a disastrous fire in 1941 consumed the mill and its stock of logs and converted timber in a spectacular conflagration. It is an ill wind, however, and the opportunity was taken, with the help and encouragement of various government departments to rebuild. The new construction was the most up-to-date sawmill in the United Kingdom. In the 1990's the sawmills were, however, demolished, and housing estates now occupy the area.

THE ACLAND
CURIO & FANCY SHOP,
MARKET PLACE, HIGH STREET,
HONITON.

H.R. Harris had two bakery premises in Honiton. One, seen here in the 1920s, was in High Street, opposite the Dolphin, where, as early as 1906, he had advertised the Central Restaurant as being 'convenient for Visitors, Tourists and Ladies and Gentleman on business'. Today the shop is Barclay's Bank. Mr Harris, who was Mayor of Honiton at one time, also made ices and jellies to order and, both here and at his other shop in East End, he had a fine name as a baker and confectioner. He delivered bread and cakes thoughout Honiton and the surrounding districts, as seen in the bottom picture, which dates from around 1899.

Four

... and Play

Honiton's High Street decked out for Queen Victoria's Diamond Jubilee in 1897. The smart appearance and youthfulness of most of the Honitonians suggests that this was no ordinary market but a gala occasion connected with the great day itself.

The Peace Celebrations (11 November 1918 was only an Armistice) outside the Market House on 19 July 1919. The firing party strikes a sombre note but Brockway's and the adjoining shop are decorated in festive style. The reading of the Peace Proclamation was followed by Children's Entertainment, and in the evening there was an open-air concert, arranged by B.P. Warren and R. Hales in the High Street.

Lower High Street, Honiton, decorated for the Silver Jubilee of King George V in 1935.

Silver Jubilee celebrations in 1935 included a monster parade, seen above, headed by the police with the civic dignitaries behind, turning west out of New Street and, presumably, turning back on itself somewhere around Gissage Bridge and then marching back up High Street (below) for a thanksgiving service in St Paul's. Of special interest above is the fine view of the old Black Lion Inn, which was closed and demolished in 1967 when the bottom of New Street was widened in the interests of traffic safety. Hoskins, on the opposite corner, a drapers, tailors and outfitters of considerable repute, is now a greengrocers shop. In the bottom picture, every branch of the town's life was found in the parade, including, in front of Frisby's Shoe Store, the railway station staff and the fire brigade.

The Silver Jubilee procession has arrived at the top of High Street and turned to march down past Plympton House and, presumably, head for St Paul's church.

Honiton Town Band heads the procession as it marches up a High Street awash with flags and bunting.

Coronation King George VI, 1937.

Two years later, in May 1937, the procession for George VI's coronation makes it way along High Street towards St Paul's church.

The letters 'H.C.C.' indicate that this special occasion on 14 June 1913 (on the scoreboard behind) is connected with Honiton Cricket Club. The clock and horseshoe on the table suggest this is a formal presentation, presumably to a member who is leaving the district.

Left: An unknown occasion in Honiton's High Street at the turn of the century. A military band is playing to a small crowd with either the banner of a local Friendly Society or a chapel. The absence of decorations rules out any Coronation or Jubilee connections.

Below: Honiton Bowling Club members J. Kenwood (left) and R.H. Kenwood (on his left) won the Devon County (East Devon Section) Pairs Competition at Budleigh Salterton on 2 June 1937. In the final they beat a Budleigh pair which included H. Carter (with pipe), the reigning Devon Singles champion.

'Loniton' cricket club 1st XI outside the pavilion on the old Allhallows Playing Field, 1940s. Back row, left to right: John Roderigo (umpire), Arthur Moore, Ralph Dart, Bob Richards, Andrew Rutherford, Fred Cann, Peter Toogood, Dick Hurford (umpire), a now unknown sports master from Gloucester Road School. Front: Geoffrey Gill, Bill Gillard, Kenneth Moore, Leslie Moore, Arthur Trim. The name 'Loniton' came from joint football and cricket teams between local boys and evacuees from the Gloucester Road School, Peckham. The London boys were excellent at football but not really interested in cricket, which is why the above team consists entirely of local boys.

Honiton Bowling Club President Mr Cottrell bowling the first wood of the season in the 1950s. Members watching include Jack Samson, Mr and Mrs Owen Cleverdon, Lionel Pate, Arthur Dimond, George Doble, Tom Bambury, Ron Carter, Hedley Parker and Stan Northcote.

Archie Dimond bowls the first wood of his year of office around the same period. Members seen here include Arthur Dimond, Sylvia Dimond, Tom and Alice Bambury, Jack Parsons, Tom Soper, Mr and Mrs George Doble, Harry Chown, Henry Lowman, Ernie Clapp, Bill Wyatt and Mr Norton.

Honiton Rugby 1st XV, 1928–29, the middle of three successive Devon Junior Cup-winning seasons for Honiton. Standing, left to right: Walt Channing, Harold Carnell, P. Lerche (sec), A. Stone, W. Baker, B. Chapman, J. Rogers, C. Hatcher, B. Nott, F. Tucker, F. Beer, M.W. Trim. Middle: C. Doble, A. Paul, E. Woodrow, E. Munt, G. Locke. Front: B. Dunsford, S. Carnell, L. Gigg, A. Wyatt.

Honiton Rugby Club, 1951–52. Back row, left to right: R. Sprake (referee), S. Stower (touch judge), G. Locke, J. Lodwig, A. Long, D. Pulman, R. Miller, W. Hill, P. Murray, R. Hill, G.R. Locke (trainer). Middle: J. Fowler, G. Fawcett (vice-capt), B. Evans (capt), J. Warren, D. Hill (sec). Front: J. Retter, M. Kenwood.

Honiton Boy Scouts' tableau in a Honiton Carnival of around 1956.

The annual concert was one of the highlights of the Summerland School's year. Here, in around 1949, the performers are, back row, left to right: Jeannette Farmer, Jean Costa, Sylvia Samsom, -?-, Mary Bambury, Joan Howells, Susan Heard. Middle: Gina Moncrieff, -?-, Sally Eveleigh, Wendy Davis. Front: -?-, -?-.

Honiton Show in the 1920s. Note that the Southern Railway (left background) even had a stand in those days.

Honiton Show c. 1924, when it was held on the Show Field. In 1940 the Heathfield Army Camp was built there and today it is an industrial park.

Honiton Fair in the old Fair Ground, 1912.

Anderton Rowland Amusement Contractors, a euphuism for fairground entertainers, at Honiton Fair in 1912.

Five

Cotley, Offwell, Wilmington and Farway

Tom Stamp says goodbye to his wife May and son Bill at Dovecot, Cotleigh, still the family's home, before going off for service with the Devonshire Regiment in World War One.

Cotleigh School. Among the pupils seen above around 1925 are Horace Netherway, Bill Stamp, Ada and Amy Cook, Vera Harris, Roy Norton and Gordon Stamp. The group below, from around 1937, is, back row, left to right: Cecil Retter, Esme Board, Winnie Pearce, Bob Stamp, Michael Wakeley. Middle: Bill Banfield, Sybil Retter, Hazel Coombes, -?-, Les Pearce. Front: Douglas Lane, Doreen Banfield, -?-, -?-, Connie Netherway, George Board. The education authorities announced their plans to close the school in 1948 but, as the result mainly of strong opposition from the village, it remained open until 1977, when, with numbers down to fourteen, it finally closed. Today Cotleigh's children go to nearby Offwell School (see opposite).

Three generations of the Stamp family at Hawkins Cottage, Cotley, in 1917. Mrs May Stamp is on the left, her son Bill on the horse, and her mother-in-law on the right. The family bought the cottage for £98 when the Cotleigh estate was sold in 1919 by the Marquis of Northampton.

Offwell school and village centre, c. 1905.

The Five Bells Inn, Offwell, *c.* 1910. The Five Bells, like so many pubs beside a parish church, takes its name from the number of bells in the peel at that church. In Offwell's case, the inn was actually in the north-east corner of St Mary's churchyard until around the turn of the century, when it was demolished. The licence was transferred to the site seen here which still happily bears the name Five Bells, although the inn was closed before World War Two.

Offwell & Widworthy Cricket Club, *c.* 1953. Back row, left to right: -?-, Des Broom, Mike Cousins, David Farmer, -?-, Roy Richards, Fred Cann, Daisy Richards (scorer). Front: Roy Land, Mike Doble, Bob Richards, M. Richards, -?-, Bob Pyne.

Offwell & Widworthy Football Club 1st XI, 1949–50. Back row, left to right: Mr Fred Bastin, A. Clarke, B. Tidball, F. Cann, F.C. Blackmore (secretary), D. Davies, M.H. Richards, M. Maughan, Mr Ackland. Front: R. Wood, A. Williams (vice-captain), J. Hudson (captain), R. Atkins, B. Perry.

Offwell & Widworthy Football Club 2nd XI, 1949–50. Back row, left to right: D. Ackland, R.N. Richards, P. Spence, D. Farmer, L. Gray, T. Connett, Mr Bastin. Front: R. Morey, V. White, L. Channon (captain), D. Batten, W. Richards.

Widworthy Barton and church, *c.* 1923. The old thatched cyder house (centre) has been demolished.

Wellington Farm, Wilmington, *c.* 1900. The trees opposite are at the entrance to Home Farm.

Rose (left) and Violet Cottages, Wilmington, *c.* 1901. Rose Cottage was subsequently demolished.

Home Farm, Wilmington, *c.* 1912. Mrs Emma Cole with two of her grandsons, William (in her arms) and his brother Leonard. Home Farm, which bears the date 1625 on a chimney, has been a hotel and restaurant since about 1950.

Wilmington Stores, *c.* 1920. Note the petrol pumps.

Wilmington Club's annual highlights were the Trinity Monday Parade to Widworthy church and the following sports and jollifications in Mr Harry Lane's field in Butchers Lane afterwards. The field was always mown early to accommodate the revellers. The parade is shown making its way towards the church in around 1924.

Wilmington children return from the annual school treat at Seaton in around 1920.

This caption may say 'Bert Cleal outside the White Hart at Wilmington around 1910', but, with due respect to Bert, he is not the star of the picture.

Seen here soon after its completion, this fountain was built at Wilmington through voluntary subscriptions to mark the Diamond Jubilee of Queen Victoria in 1897.

Wilmington School, c. 1924. Back row, left to right: Frank Broom, Elsie Heard, Lilian North, ? Langford, Fred Batten, ? Brice, Annie Broom, May Tratt, Wilfred Cummings. Front: Fred Hutchings, Fred Broom, Cyril Henley, Gladys Wood, Joyce Godfrey, Winnie Godfrey, Peter Evans, Ivy Hurford, Percy Godfrey, Ray Griffin. The school closed in the late 1940s.

Right: Millhead Cottage, Farway, *c.* 1904. Called Millhead in earlier nineteenth-century times, a name it has since reverted to, the cottage was known as Thorn Farm for a few years.

Below: Oak View, Farway, *c.* 1901. Farway, a scattered hamlet to the south-east of Honiton, takes its name from 'faer-weg', the frequented way – possibly a reference to the old track that led to the flints on Beer Head. These have been worked since the dawn of Devon's history, either from Hembury Fort, near Broadhembury, or by the middle Bronze Age people who used the hills above Farway for their burial grounds.

Annings, the old blacksmiths shop in Farway, in around 1900.

Farway United Football Club, Perry Street League Intermediate (South) champions, 1949–50.
Back row, left to right: S.F. Lee (treasurer), B.N. Selway, L. James, W. Baily, E.J. Hooper, F.
Loud, W. Charlton, M. Bunney (committee). Front: C.J. Northcote, R. Berry, E. Berry (capt),
John Baily (mascot in front), D.D. Selway, E. Fowler. Then, as now, Farway Football Club was
a very home-grown affair. And it is worth recalling that the club ended the 1994–95 season by
winning promotion, as Division One runners-up, to the Perry Street League's Premier Division
for the first time ever, with another largely home-grown side, and that, remarkably for such a
small community, it runs two teams.

Robert Lee serving petrol at Cox's Villa (now Cottage), Farway, in the 1920s.

Farway Home Guard during World War Two. Back row, left to right: Roger Wood, Harry Batten, Jack Webber, Cedric Summers, Ernie Baily, Tom Spurway. Second row: Sam Reed, Brian Lane, Nick Reed, Jack Batten, ? Sweetland, -?-, Bob Summers, Wilfred Payne. Third row: Stan Lane, Jim Price, Bob Newbery, ? Parris, Gordon Snell, Tony Tett, Tom Berry. Front: Geoff Norman, Philip Mitchell, Albert Sweetlnd, Fred Holland, Leonard Milhead, George Tucker, Jack Spiller, Ern Goddard.

Farway 1953 Coronation Harvest Home. Among those seen here are George Wood, Frank Loud, Don Lee and Arthur Banks.

Farway Methodist Church Sunday School, c. 1904. Prior to 1895 the Methodist community had worshipped at Goldacre Farm, just around the corner from the chapel which had been built at a cost of £397 by John Wakeley, a stonemason from nearby Northleigh. It was designed by the well-known architect Robert Curwen, who received twenty-four pounds and, with economy in mind, designed three local chapels in the same L-shape. Those at Otterton and Farway were a left-handed L, the one at Colaton Raleigh right-handed. Much of the money for the building at Farway was raised locally and Mrs Annie Wood, the first member to be married there and, at 91, the oldest member and still living nearby, remembers the old oil lamps being filled by a lady using a tea pot. People thought nothing in earlier days of walking the five miles from Honiton for chapel events.

Six

Monkton, Combe Raleigh, Luppitt and Dunkeswell

John Gosling was head gardener at Halsdon House, between Beacon and Monkton, when this picture was taken in 1906. He later moved to Seaton. Left to right: John Gosling with Elizabeth (Cissie) on his lap, John (junior), Mary (behind), Elizabeth Gosling (nee Totterdell) with Jim on her lap, and Tom.

MONKTON VILLAGE. NEAR HONITON.

Modern day Monkton (seen here in around 1906) is plagued by heavy summer traffic which makes life a misery as it thunders along the A30 trunk road. Happily, a by-pass is planned to link up with Honiton's. The village gets its name from 'Monks' Farm' and was once part of the royal demesne and a chapelry of Honiton. The church of St Mary Magdalene, seen below, was virtually completely rebuilt in 1863 but it is still an attractive little building. Some Morris windows and stencilling in the nave are of particular interest.

Monkton, near Honiton.

36

Right: Combe Raleigh, *c.* 1905. The village takes its name from Sir Walter's ancestors, who lived here during the thirteenth century.

Below: St Nicholas's church, Combe Raleigh, *c.* 1909. Although its list of rectors goes back as far as 1260, St Nicholas's church dates mainly from the fourteenth (the tower) or the fifteenth century (the nave, chancel and north aisle).

Honiton, Combe Raleigh Church.

Luppitt Post Office, c. 1902.

The Red Lion Inn, Luppitt, c. 1900. Today the inn is called Luppitt Inn and its entrance is at the back, where the bar is among the smallest in England. Its licence dates from at least 1890 and three generations of the Wright family, Charles, Bill and Alb, were landlords. Alb was followed as licensee by his widow Mary.

Newhouse Farm, Luppitt, *c.* 1904.

The Barn, Luppitt, at the turn of the century, when the cattle seen here were milked where they stood in the muddy yard.

Left: Luppitt School and Schoolhouse, *c.* 1900. Closed and now a private residence, the village school stood towards the top of the steep hill that was Luppitt's 'main street'. Near its top, and commanding fine views down the valley, St Mary's church is among Devon's better village churches and well worth a visit if only for the fine wagon roof inside.

Below: Dowlish Farm, Luppitt, *c.* 1904.

Dowlish Farm, Luppitt.

Tapswater, Luppitt, c. 1910.

The Chapel, Beacon, Luppitt, c. 1900. Beacon, pronounced 'Becon', was, and is, a tiny hamlet between Luppitt and Monkton. The chapel, now a private residence, was supported by a wide area. Although many obviously did come by carriage, and on horseback, many worshippers walked long distances, in rain, snow and worse, two and sometimes three times on Sundays.

Luppitt Manor Court Leet, held at the Luppitt Inn on 29 November 1937. Standing, left to right: T. Thorn, J. Richards, F. Bartlett, W. Stevens, A.E. Summers, T. Wilson. Seated: J.F. Madge, C.N. Wright, John Madge, J. Crabb, F. Valentine, A. Clapp.

The ladies cricket team for Luppitt Festival Week in May 1949, pictured outside the Luppitt Inn. It included Mary Wright, Winnie Rowland, Annie Corrick, Olive Clapp, Lily Pulman, Hazel Norton, Peggy Rosewell and Nancy Crabb.

The Smithy, Dunkeswell, *c.* 1910. The building, long since converted into a private home, still stands at the foot of the village's main street.

Dunkeswell School, *c.* 1910. To its immediate left, with the badge above the door, was the police station; to its left was the post office. The school became the village hall in 1953 (see p.108).

Dunkeswell, c. 1899.

The ceremony to mark the opening of Dunkeswell Village Hall in 1953. Among the official party, which includes the parish council are: Mr A.G. Le Marchant, Mr W. Farmer, Mr J. Richards, Mr L. Proctor, Mrs M. Broad, Mrs E. Gollop, Mrs E. Belchner, Mrs V. Eley, Miss E. Proctor, Revd R.H. Vokes, Mr M.R. Cox, Mr F. Wells and Mr F. Talbot.

Seven

Awliscombe, Feniton, Fennybridges and Gittisham

Weston, the tiny hamlet to the west of Honiton, c. 1910. The name comes from the Old English (Anglo-Saxon) west tun or 'west farm'.

The Otter Inn, Weston, c.1939.

The Carpenter's Arms, Weston, seen here in around 1888, was closed around 1900. Pictures of the building in 1905 show that the smithy on the left of the inn was not only closed, but had also been demolished. The Carpenter's Arms was a fully-licensed inn; its near neighbour the Otter was only a cyder house.

Awliscombe *en fête* for the coronation of King George VI in 1937.

Godford Mill, Awliscombe, *c.* 1889. Run by Geoffrey Rounsevell, the mill also had a baker's shop (out of sight to the right) from which bread was delivered throughout the district by the carts seen here.

Awliscombe School, *c.* 1908.

Awliscombe Post Office at Cooper's Cottages in 1926. Sadly, perhaps, the lovely old thatched cottages were demolished, and today the village hall's car park occupies the site.

Losses Farm, Awliscombe, seen above on the left around the turn of the century, had lost its thatch by the time the bottom picture was taken, probably no more than ten years later. Buffetts, the house in the middle background, has fallen into disrepair in that short time. The timber wagon shows the extent to which a rural community still depended on real horse-power. Everything, including much heavier loads than this, was moved by horses.

Awliscombe bell ringers at St Michael's and All Angels' church, Awliscombe, *c.* 1908. Left to right: Dick Franks, Jack Bishop, Fred Heath, Albion Dyer (sexton), Bill Bishop, Tom Anthony, Tom Larcombe.

St Michael and All Angels' church, Awliscombe, *c.* 1905. The church stands on a small knoll, on an ancient holy site where tradition places a pagan temple. Although it has a few Norman remains, the church is mainly fifteenth-century. A peculiarity is the pronounced upward slope of the nave.

Buckerell, seen here in around 1900, is typical of the villages that cluster along the foot of the Blackdown Hills. It gave its name to an Andrew Bokerel who was seven times Lord Mayor of London.

Feniton, c. 1910.

Feniton, c. 1909.

Feniton, c. 1906. Modern Feniton is really two separate villages: old Feniton, an attractive place clustered around St Andrew's church and with more than its fair share of cobb and thatch; and the other half which has grown up around the former Sidmouth Junction railway station, closed by Beeching but re-opened as Feniton as housing mushroomed around it.

The Greyhound Inn at Fennybridges near Honiton, seen here in around 1901, took its name from the London coach that changed horses here. It was almost destroyed by fire in 1968 but an admirable lookalike replaced it four years later.

Bloomfield Guest House, Fennybridges, near Honiton, in the 1920s, now the Fennybridges Inn. It was around the bridge just a few yards along the road that a decisive action in the Prayer Book Rebellion of 1549 took place. The rebels, incensed over Cranmer's insistence they use the new Prayer Book, held the bridge against Lord Russell's government army, who eventually won the day but only after a bloody battle.

Coaches waiting outside the Greyhound Hotel at Fennybridges in the late 1920s.

The Forge, Fennybridges, *c.* 1924. The Dommett family were blacksmiths here from the early nineteenth century until the 1950s.

Fairmile Inn, Escot, c. 1907, said sometimes to get its name from its being 'a fair mile from Ottery', and sometimes from this being a stretch of road which is particularly easy. A more romantic story tells of a Cavalier chased out of Ottery by Oliver Cromwell, who, on reaching the inn, collapsed, gasping 'I have led you a fair mile'.

The Beech Walk above Gittisham, seen here in around 1907, was planted by the lawyer Thomas Putt when he came to Combe House in 1757. But Putt's name is probably best remembered by the world at large for the Tom Putt apple. Which Tom Putt introduced the famous cyder apple, however, is open to question. There were several in the family, including one who became vicar of Farway towards the end of the eighteenth century whose claim is advanced in a stained glass window in St Michael's church.

Gittisham, *c.* 1920. This card was 'published' (i.e. sold) by H. Bowyer, the Post Office, Gittisham. The bakery in the left background was run by John Haymes for many years until he retired in the early 1950s. Jim Eveleigh took over and was followed in turn by his son, another Jim. Sadly the business was closed in the early 1990s and Gittisham is now without a baker.

Gittisham Rectory, *c.* 1939. Now demolished, probably its most striking reminder of former glories to a first-time visitor to the village is a particularly handsome red rhododendron, a survivor from the gardens.

Gittisham, *c.* 1930.

Waterside, Gittisham, *c.* 1935. A particularly attractive village, with more than its fair share of thatch, Gittisham is blessed with St Michael's, a fine parish church dating from a partial rebuilding in 1321. Inside there are particularly handsome (if overpowering) box pews (1715) and a fine wagon-roof with purling beams and small bosses.

Gittisham, *c.* 1920.

Gittisham School, *c.* 1928. Back row, left to right: Olive Marks, Grace Edwards, Vera Solman, Lil Abbott, Nancy Heath, -?-, -?-. Middle: -?-, -?-, Margaret Selway, Perry Gray, Annie Rowe, -?-, -?-, Lena Rowe. No names survive for the front row.

The Abbott cousins at Goldcombe Farm, Gittisham, in the early 1920s. Left to right: Walt, Jack, Frances and Dick.

Group B, Gittisham School, c. 1931. Back row, left to right: Walt Dominy, Arthur Rowe, Walter Gray, Arthur Heath, Fred Blackmore. Middle: Ralph Solman, Gladys Gray, -?-, Margaret Knobbs, Betty Isaac, Betty Solman, -?-, Joan Humphries, Miss Salter. Front: -?-, Rita Edwards, Maureen Hayman, Joyce Bunney, Brenda Perry. Gittisham School has been closed since 1948, the children being bussed to Feniton.

Gittisham and Honiton Home Guard members during World War Two include Jack Abbott, Jim Thompson, Albert Heath, Dick Bright, Les Isaac and Alf Partridge.

A Gittisham School children's tea party in the Village Hall, c. 1958. Among those enjoying themselves are Denis Abbott, Miss Nicholas (teacher), Mrs Bunny, Connie Donnely, Valerie Chown, Clive and Celia Partridge, Brian Chown, Michael Isaac, Michael Clark, Martin Raynor, Roy Abbott and Jean Heath.

Gittisham St John Ambulance Brigade in the Village Hall, c. 1955. Left to right: -?-, Mrs de la Pryme, Ronald Hutchinson, Ann Heath, Len Abbott, Ruth Hutchinson, Raymond Abbott, Marlene Hounsell, Andy Hutchinson, Denis Abbott, Christine Down, Stan Hutchinson, -?-.

'Tip-Tip-Toeing', an old Gittisham tradition, has the children of the village going around the boundaries of the old parish and shouting at every door: 'Tip! Tip! Toe! Please Give a Penny and Away We Go.' Here, in 1959, Mrs Brenda Abbot gives her penny to a crowd of children, including Denis, Len, Roy, Bobby, Raymond, Susan and Wendy Abbott, Clive and Celia Partridge, Slyvia Clark, Gordon Phillips, Ruth Hutchings, Robert Dominy, Sheila Harris, Steve and Martin Raynor, Anne Heath and Michael Hounsell.

Gittisham Football Club, seen here in 1955-56 with the Ottery & District League championship cup, the Golesworthy Cup, the Otter Cup and the Charity Cup, was formed in 1946 with Dick Bright (seen here) a founder member. He was treasurer from 1948 to 1976 and played, often with his four sons, until injury forced him to retire aged 49. Back row, left to right: Ray Hutchings, Bill Turner, Cecil Partridge (secretary), Jack Brokenshaw, Eddie Bright, Dick Bright, Tom Bright, Walt Dominy. Middle: Jim Turner, Keith Mitchell, Roy Bright, Bert Maers, Maurice Gray. Front: Merv Bright, Dick Turner.

Opposite above: Gittisham Football Club, c. 1948. Back row, left to right: Jack Dominy, Dick Bright, -?-, Roy Bright, Ray Dominy, Cecil Partridge. Middle: -?-, Tony Bright, Albert Heath. Front: Ron Mayne, Walt Dominy, Gilbert Lovering, Austin Clark, Des Clark.

Opposite below: Gittisham WI's 21st Birthday Party in the Village Hall in 1951. Among members present are Margaret Marks, May Rew, Enid Mitchell, Miss Champnes, Mrs Thompson, Mrs Crocker (secretary), Mrs Raymond Marker (President) and Mrs Emily Abbott.

WELCOME
TO OUR
21ST
BIRTHDAY PARTY

HONITON LACE MAKER
&LACE

Acknowledgements

We are deep in debt to Allhallows Museum for permission to use many pictures from their archives. A visit to the museum is a must for anyone interested in local history in general and Honiton's lace industry in particular. Pictures from the Museum can be found on pages 9-13, 16, 25-28, 32-33, 37, 40-41, 43, 47, 49, 50-51, 53, 56, 58, 60, 67, 72, 74-75, 77-78, 83-84, 100, 116-117.

Our thanks also go to Nan Steel for access to her fine Honiton collection and for her admirable introduction, and to the others who allowed us to borrow their treasured photographs and sometimes sent us on our way refreshed with tea and coffee.

They are: Brenda Abbott, Len Acutt, Fred Batten, Joyce Berry, George Blay Ltd, Mollie Burnell, Eddie Bright, Richard Broad, John and Valerie Cann, Arthur Dimond and Honiton Bowling Club, Bob Du Pontet, Joan Evans, John Godfrey of the Seaton Book Centre, Peter Harris, Merv Joslin, Simon Lake, Roy Land, Jean Lear, Keith Luxton of T.D. Hussey & Son, Albert Manley, Margaret Marks, Syd Middleton, Doreen Newton (née Bambury), Clive and Ada Partridge, Dave Pulman, Paul and Jennifer Redvers of the Honiton Pottery Shop, Dave Rew, Jane Sheppard, Bill Snell, Annie Wood and Mary Wright of the Luppitt Inn.

In a different direction we are grateful to the staff at Nonsuch Publishing for putting up with us, especially Simon Thraves, and to our wives, Jean and Violet, not only for putting up with us, but for suffering the disruption to their well-ordered lives.